GRAPHIC MYTHICAL HEROES

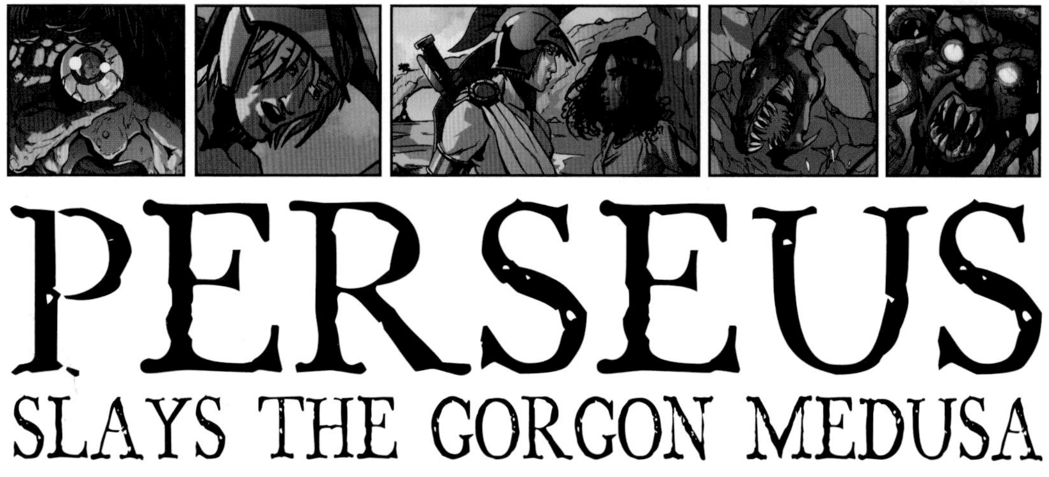

PERSEUS
SLAYS THE GORGON MEDUSA

BY GARY JEFFREY
ILLUSTRATED BY JOHN AGGS

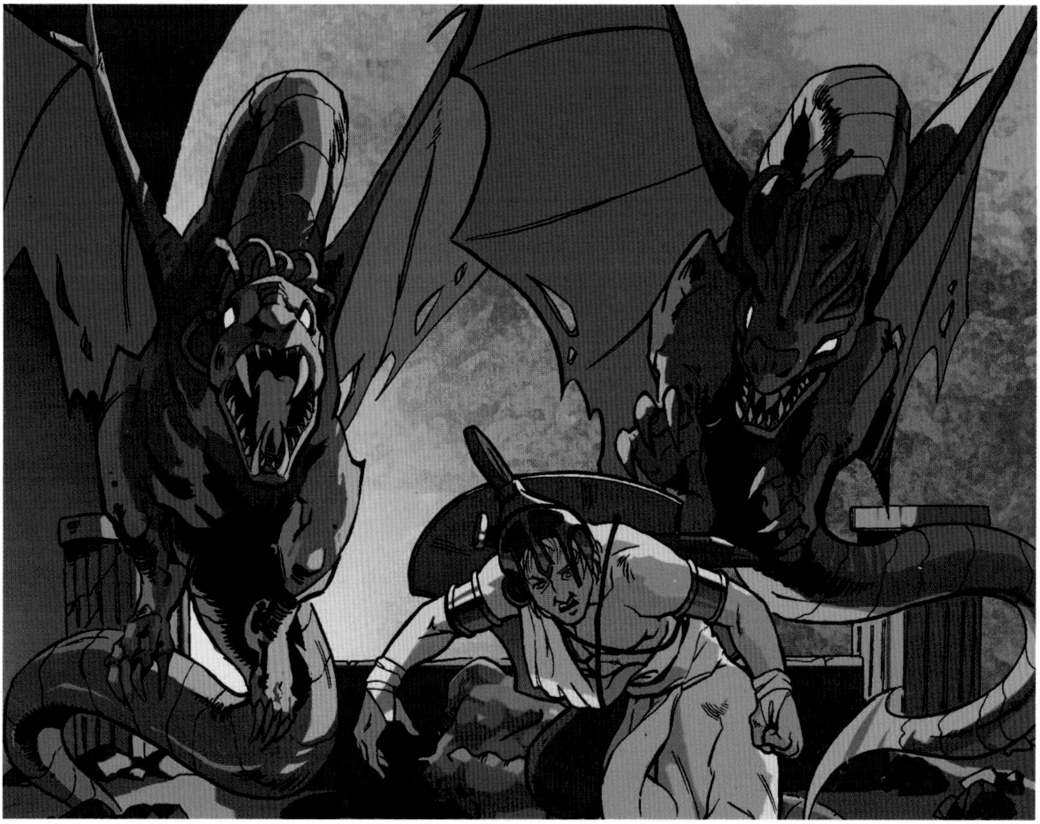

Gareth Stevens
Publishing

Please visit our website, www.garethstevens.com.
For a free color catalog of all our high-quality books,
call toll free 1-800-542-2595 or fax 1-877-542-2596.

Library of Congress Cataloging-in-Publication Data

Jeffrey, Gary.
Perseus slays the Gorgon Medusa / Gary Jeffrey.
p. cm. — (Graphic mythical heroes)
Includes index.
ISBN 978-1-4339-7524-0 (pbk.)
ISBN 978-1-4339-7525-7 (6-pack)
ISBN 978-1-4339-7523-3 (library binding)
1. Perseus (Greek mythology)—Juvenile literature. 2. Medusa (Greek
mythology)—Juvenile literature. I. Title.
BL820.P5J44 2012
398.20938'02—dc23
2012000226

First Edition

Published in 2013 by
Gareth Stevens Publishing
111 East 14th Street, Suite 349
New York, NY 10003

Designed by David West Books

Printed in China

CPSIA compliance information: Batch #DWS12GS: For further information contact Gareth Stevens, New York, New York at 1-800-542-2595.

CONTENTS

HEROIC DESTROYER

A prophet told Acrisius, the king of Argos, that one day his daughter, Danae, would bear a son. The prophet said that when this son was grown, he would kill Acrisius and take his kingdom.

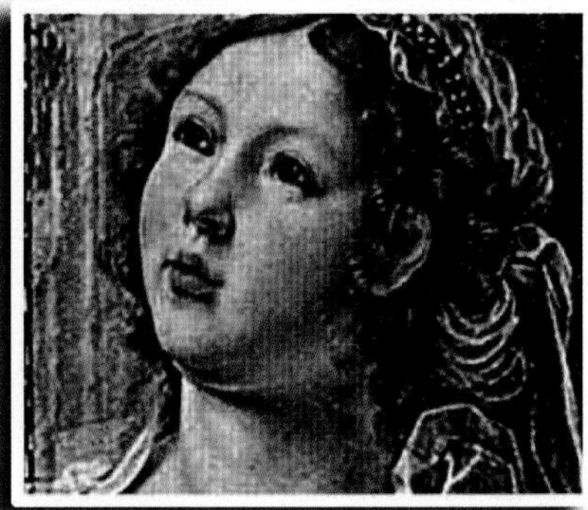

Danae named her son Perseus, which means "destroyer."

GOLDEN TOWER

Acrisius became afraid and locked Danae in a tower to keep her pure. Zeus visited the tower disguised as a shower of gold dust, and soon Danae gave birth to a boy. When Acrisius found out, he became enraged, but rather than kill Zeus's son, he sent mother and child out to sea in a chest in the hope that they would perish.

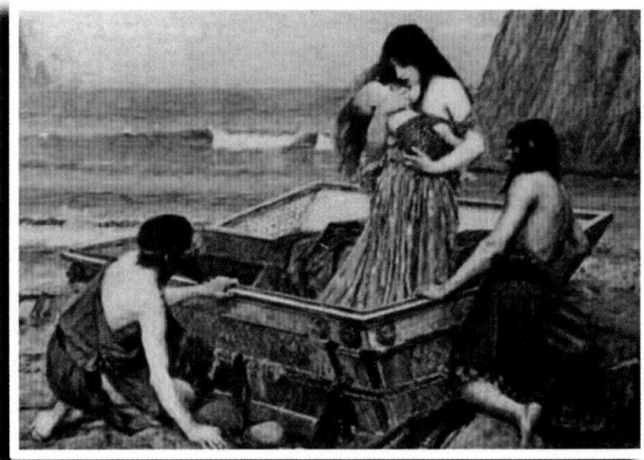

Danae and Perseus washed up on the island of Seriphos and were taken in by a fisherman called Dictys.

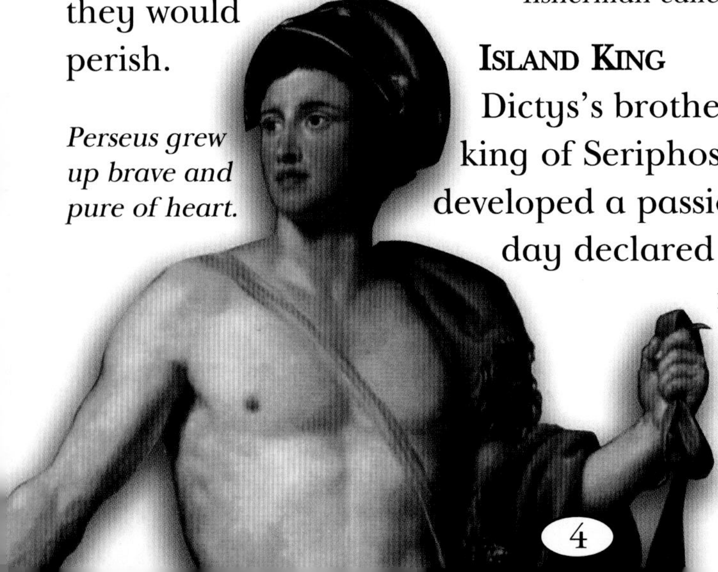

Perseus grew up brave and pure of heart.

ISLAND KING

Dictys's brother was Polydectes, the king of Seriphos. Over time, Polydectes developed a passion for Danae and one day declared that he wanted to marry her. Danae was unwilling, and Perseus, now a man, swore to protect her from Polydectes's attentions.

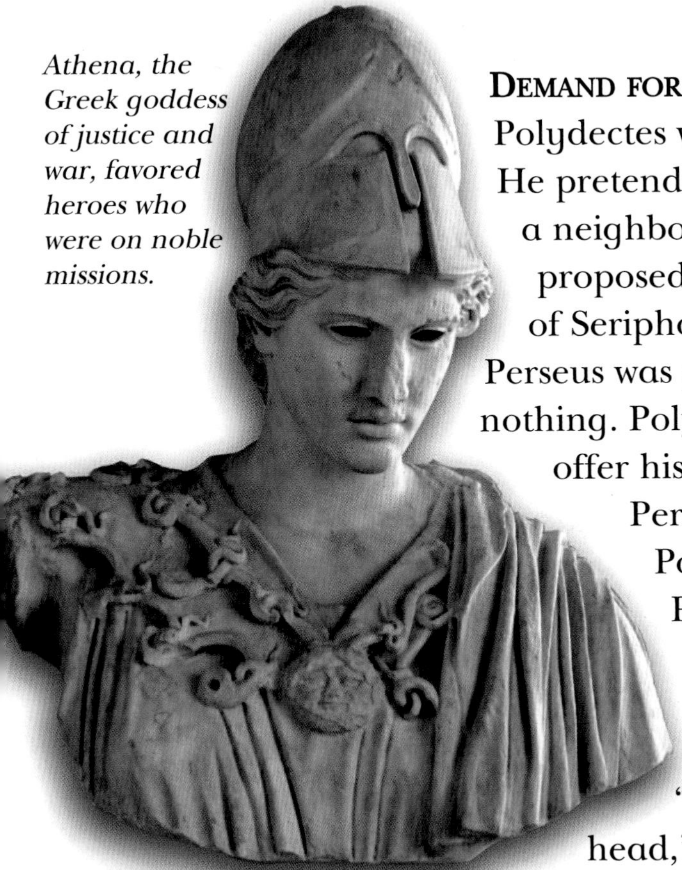

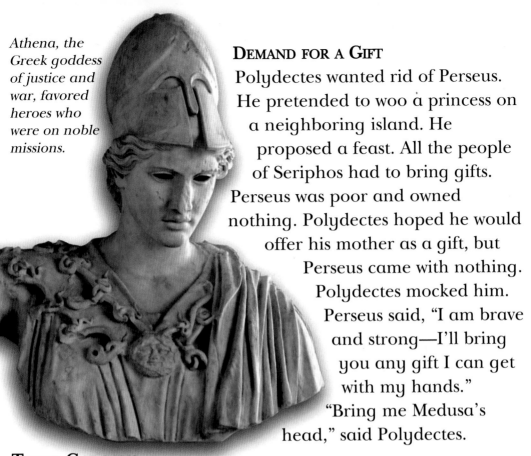

Athena, the Greek goddess of justice and war, favored heroes who were on noble missions.

Demand for a Gift

Polydectes wanted rid of Perseus. He pretended to woo a princess on a neighboring island. He proposed a feast. All the people of Seriphos had to bring gifts. Perseus was poor and owned nothing. Polydectes hoped he would offer his mother as a gift, but Perseus came with nothing. Polydectes mocked him. Perseus said, "I am brave and strong—I'll bring you any gift I can get with my hands."

"Bring me Medusa's head," said Polydectes.

Three Gorgons

Medusa was one of three sisters cursed by Athena for disrespecting her temple. She turned the once-beautiful women into hideous monsters with snakes for hair and eyes that could turn the living into stone. When Athena heard of Perseus's quest, she appeared to him and told him how to find the Gorgons and how to kill Medusa. Athena wanted the Gorgon's head to decorate her breastplate...

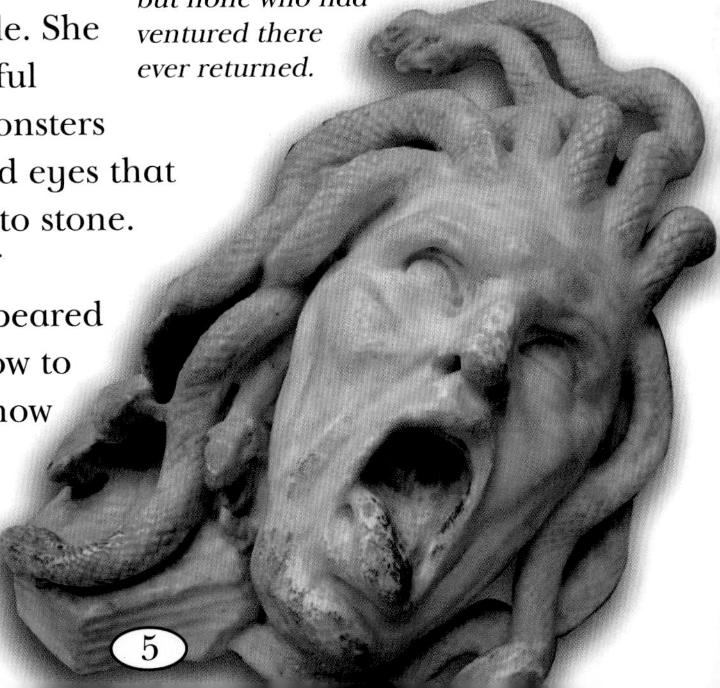

The Gorgons were rumored to live on the edge of the underworld, but none who had ventured there ever returned.

Perseus Slays the Gorgon Medusa

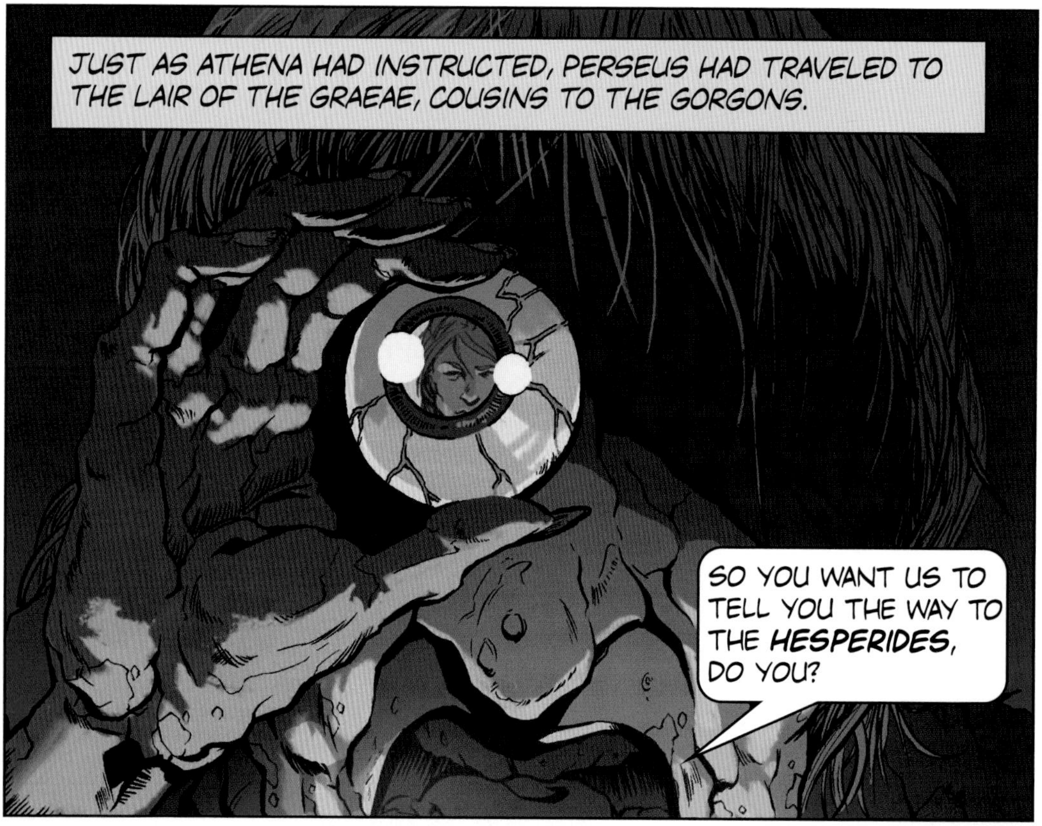
JUST AS ATHENA HAD INSTRUCTED, PERSEUS HAD TRAVELED TO THE LAIR OF THE GRAEAE, COUSINS TO THE GORGONS.
SO YOU WANT US TO TELL YOU THE WAY TO THE **HESPERIDES**, DO YOU?

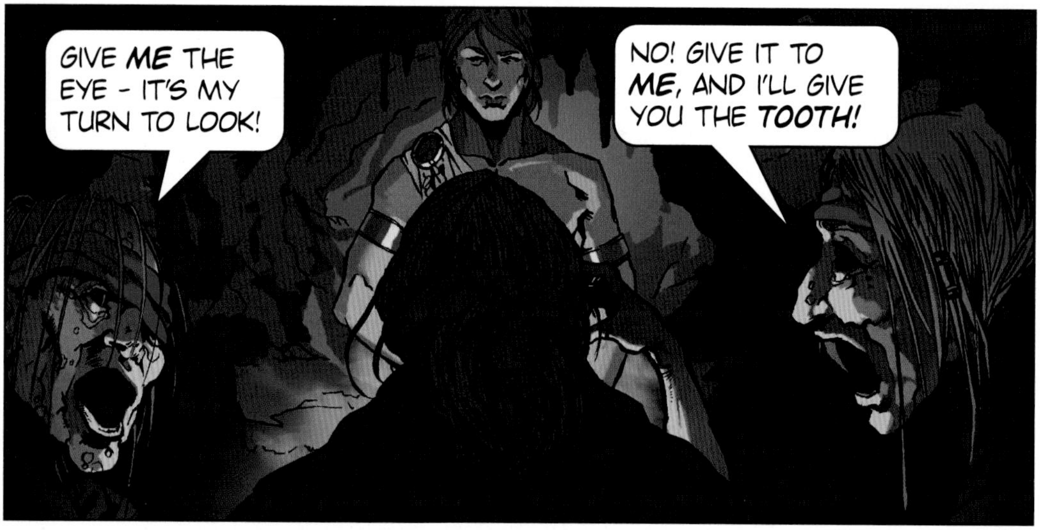
GIVE **ME** THE EYE - IT'S MY TURN TO LOOK!
NO! GIVE IT TO **ME**, AND I'LL GIVE YOU THE **TOOTH**!

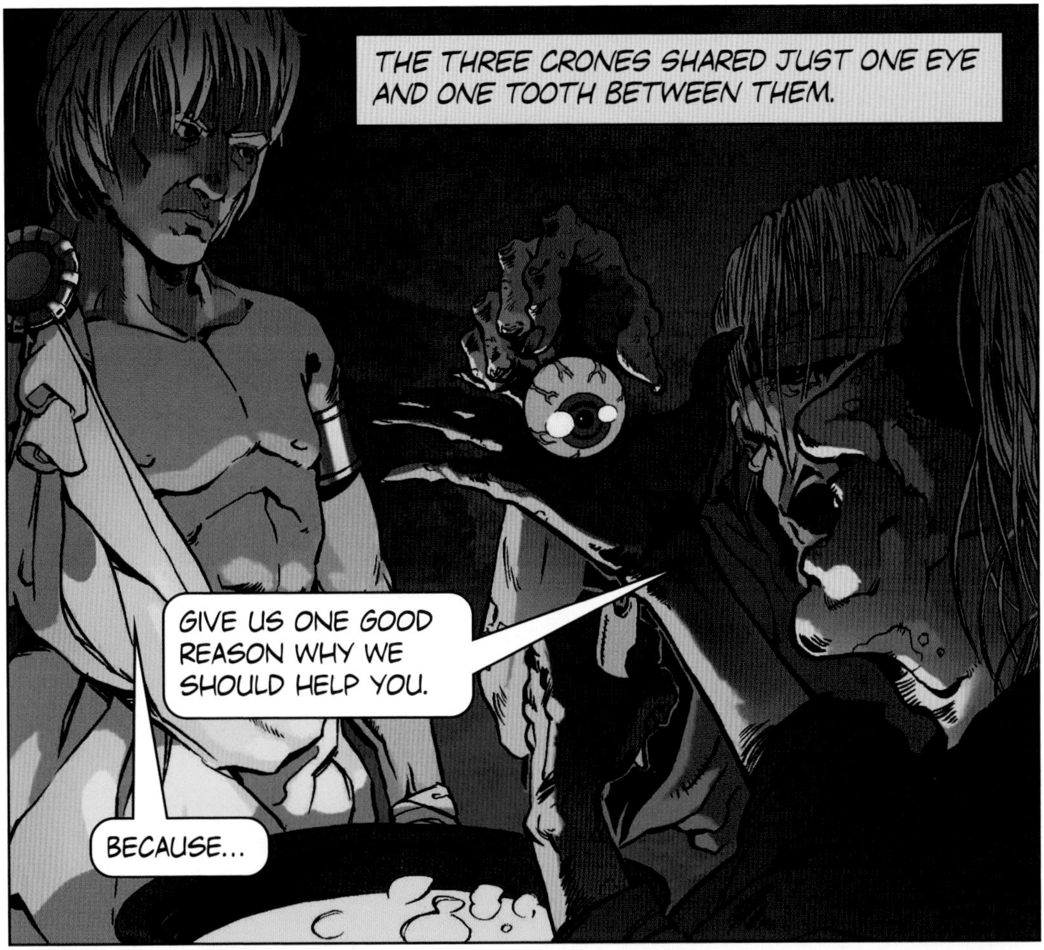
THE THREE CRONES SHARED JUST ONE EYE AND ONE TOOTH BETWEEN THEM.
GIVE US ONE GOOD REASON WHY WE SHOULD HELP YOU.
BECAUSE...

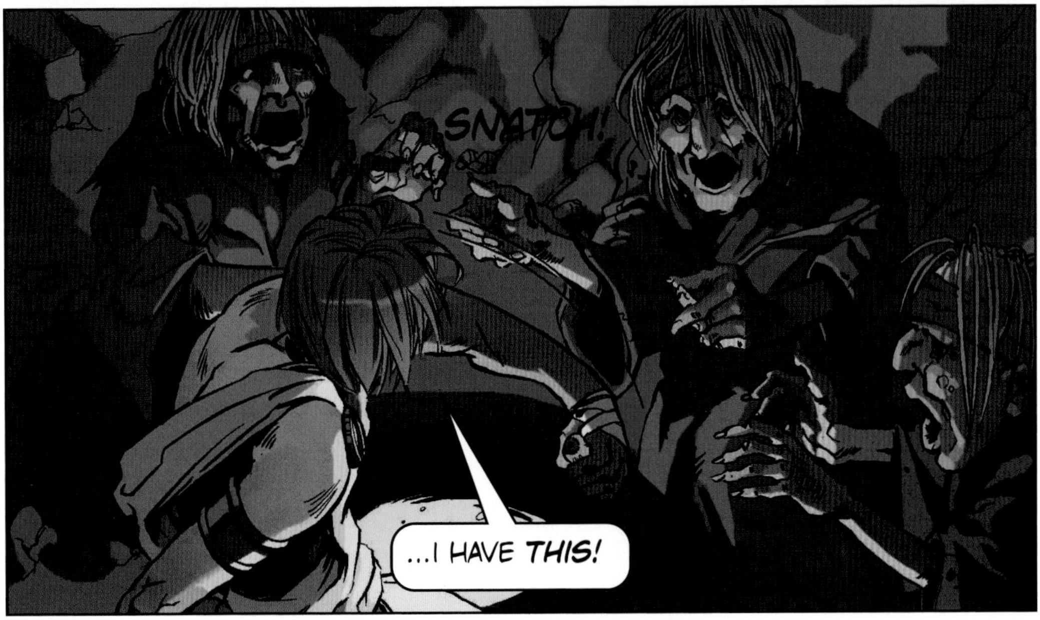
SNATCH!
...I HAVE THIS!

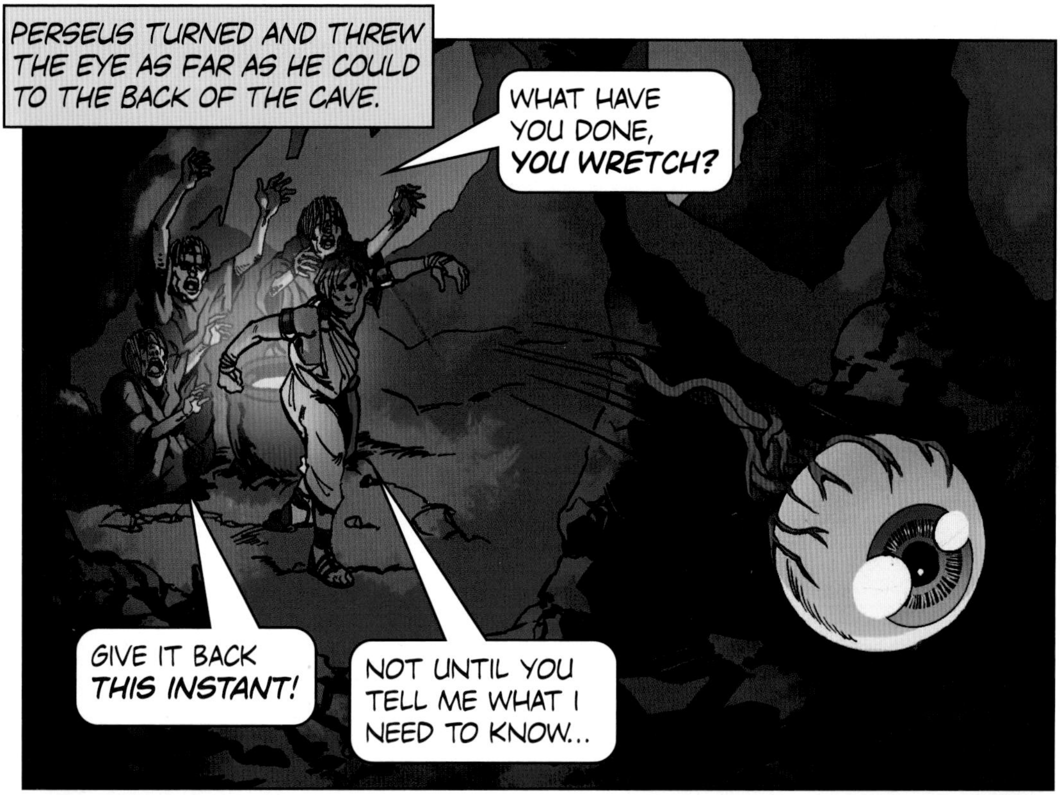
PERSEUS TURNED AND THREW THE EYE AS FAR AS HE COULD TO THE BACK OF THE CAVE.
WHAT HAVE YOU DONE, **YOU WRETCH?**
GIVE IT BACK **THIS INSTANT!**
NOT UNTIL YOU TELL ME WHAT I NEED TO KNOW...

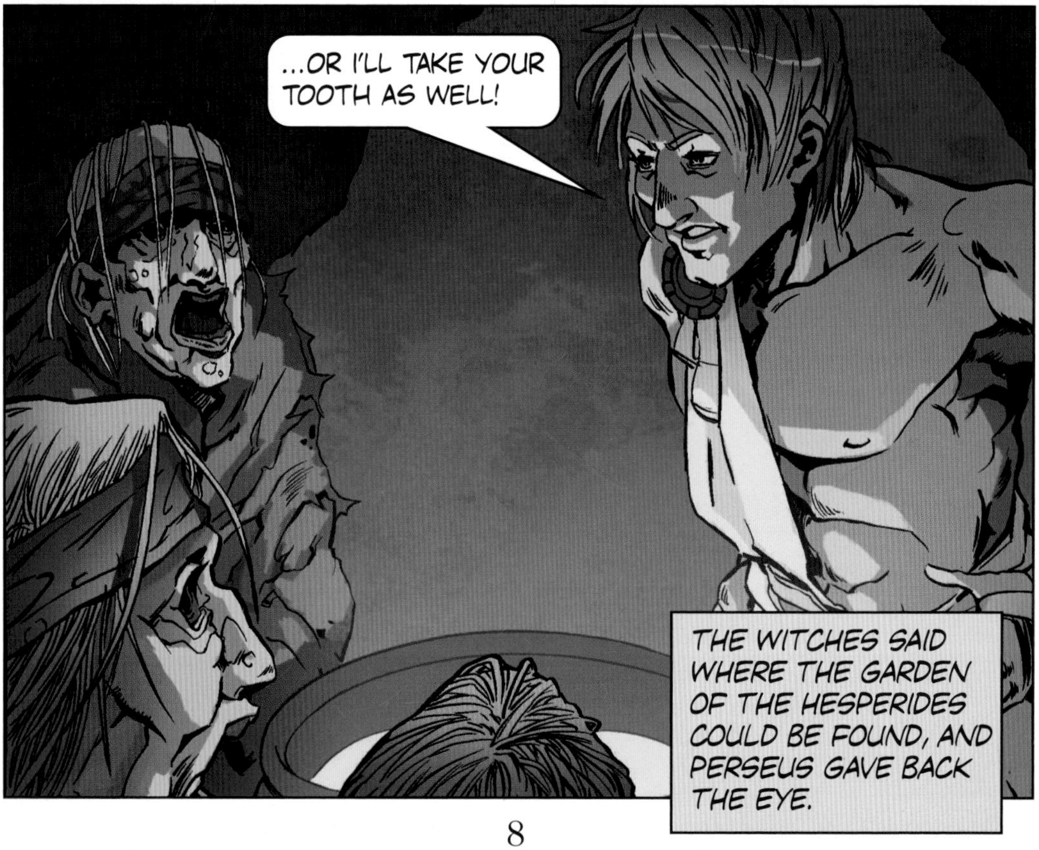
...OR I'LL TAKE YOUR TOOTH AS WELL!
THE WITCHES SAID WHERE THE GARDEN OF THE HESPERIDES COULD BE FOUND, AND PERSEUS GAVE BACK THE EYE.

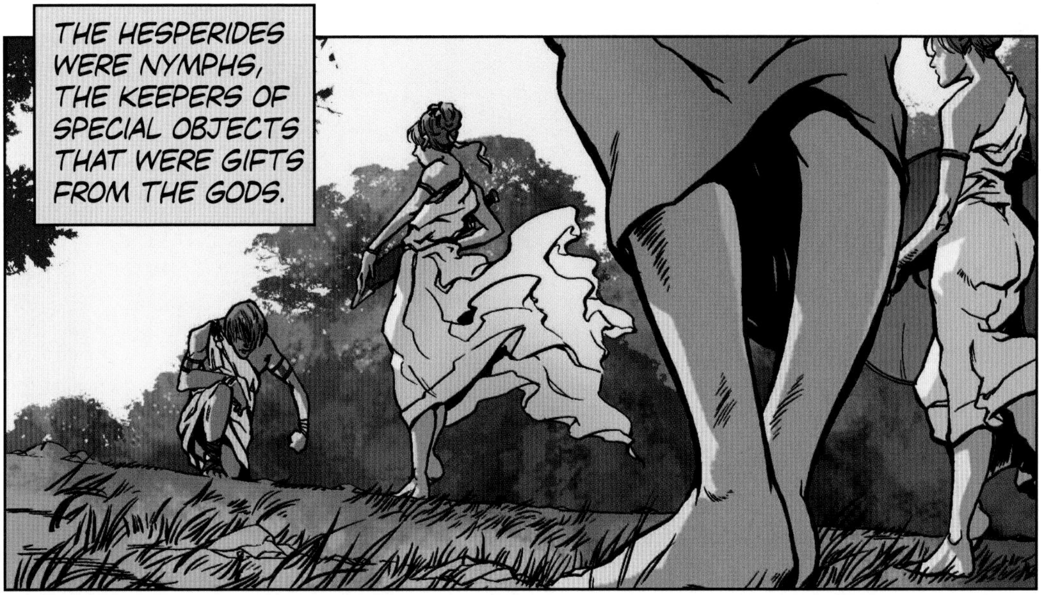
THE HESPERIDES WERE NYMPHS, THE KEEPERS OF SPECIAL OBJECTS THAT WERE GIFTS FROM THE GODS.

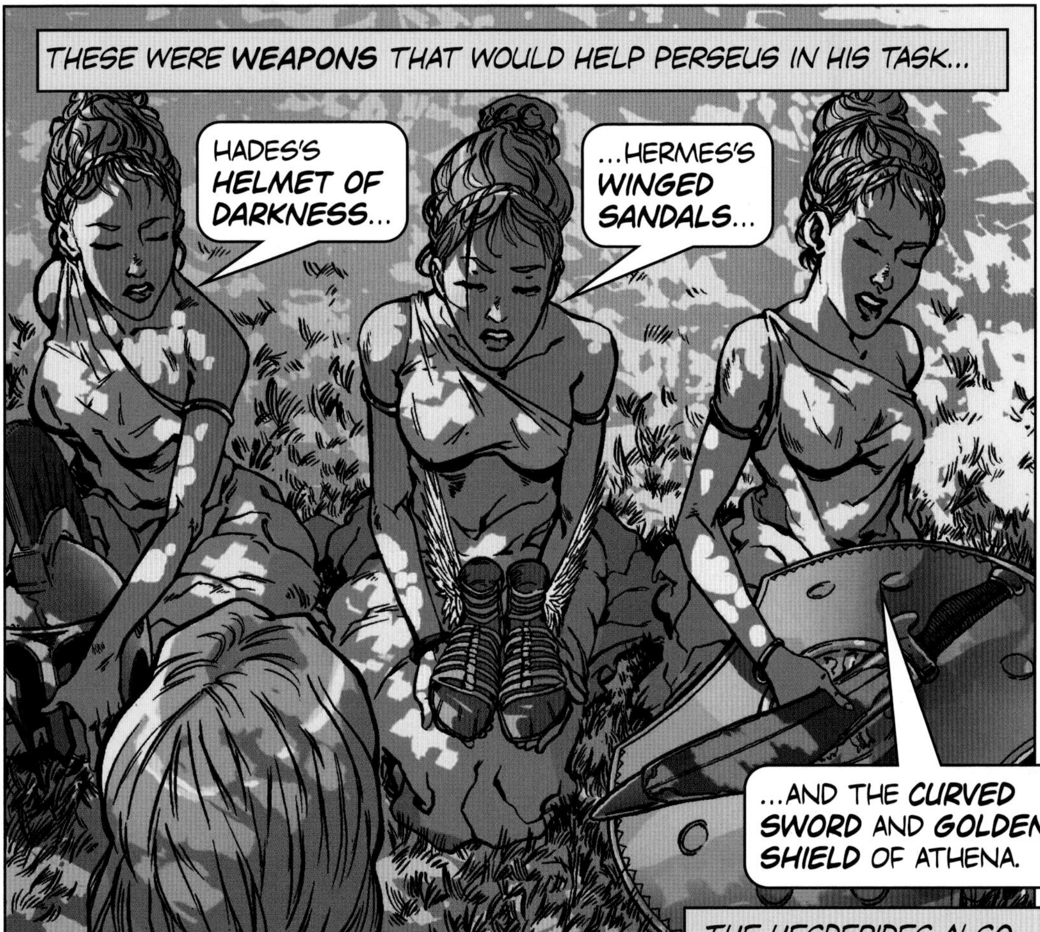
THESE WERE WEAPONS THAT WOULD HELP PERSEUS IN HIS TASK...
HADES'S HELMET OF DARKNESS...
...HERMES'S WINGED SANDALS...
...AND THE CURVED SWORD AND GOLDEN SHIELD OF ATHENA.
THE HESPERIDES ALSO PROVIDED A SPECIAL SACK FOR MEDUSA'S HEAD.

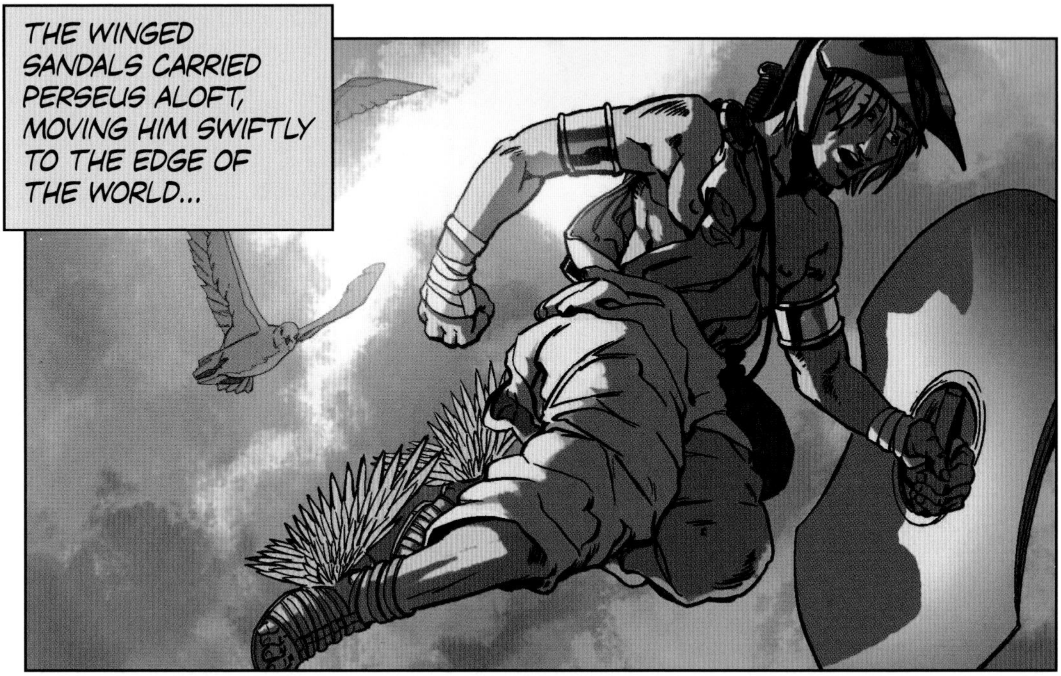
THE WINGED SANDALS CARRIED PERSEUS ALOFT, MOVING HIM SWIFTLY TO THE EDGE OF THE WORLD...

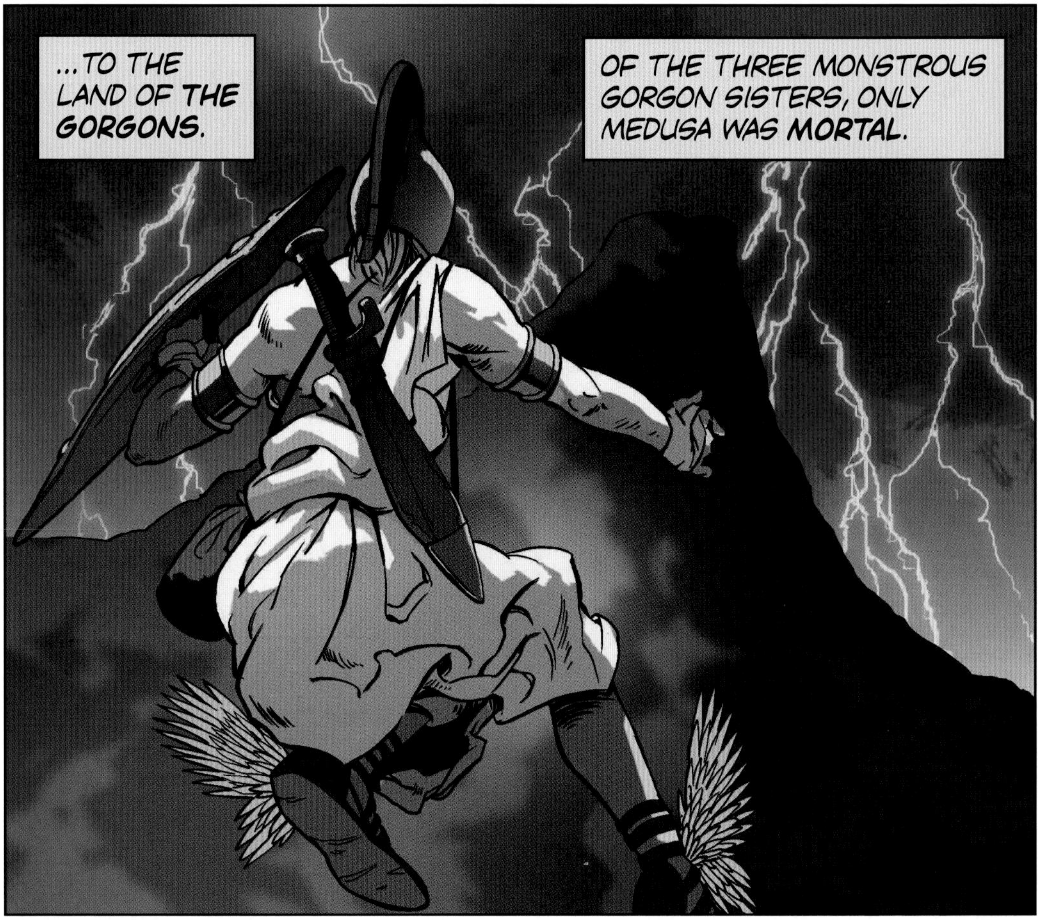
...TO THE LAND OF THE GORGONS.
OF THE THREE MONSTROUS GORGON SISTERS, ONLY MEDUSA WAS MORTAL.

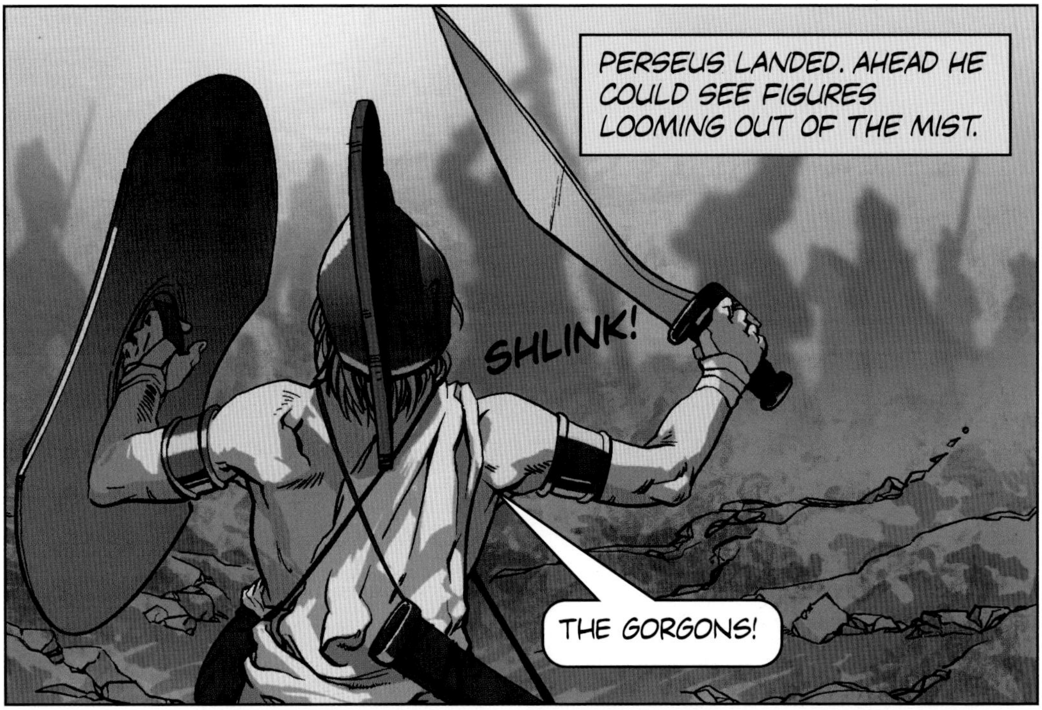
PERSEUS LANDED. AHEAD HE COULD SEE FIGURES LOOMING OUT OF THE MIST.
SHLINK!
THE GORGONS!

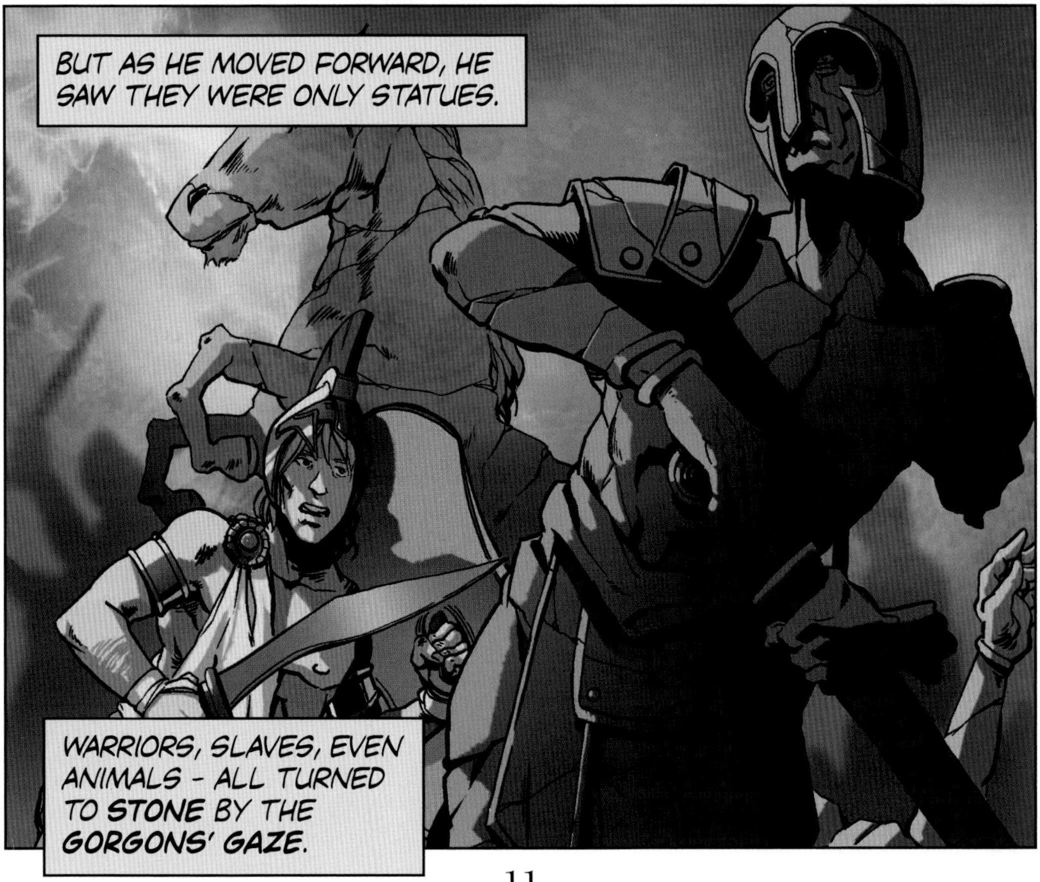
BUT AS HE MOVED FORWARD, HE SAW THEY WERE ONLY STATUES.
WARRIORS, SLAVES, EVEN ANIMALS - ALL TURNED TO **STONE** BY THE **GORGONS' GAZE**.

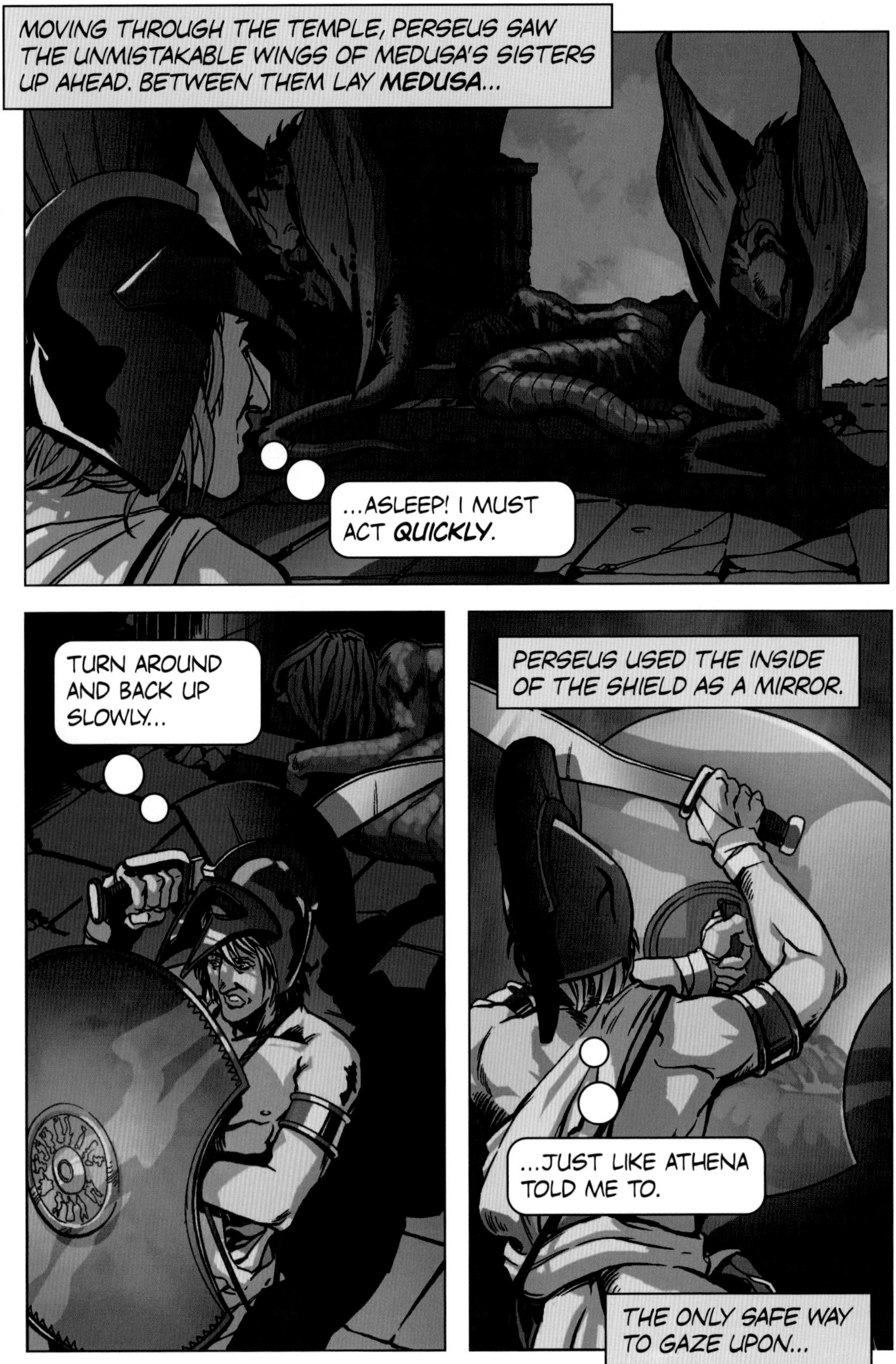
MOVING THROUGH THE TEMPLE, PERSEUS SAW THE UNMISTAKABLE WINGS OF MEDUSA'S SISTERS UP AHEAD. BETWEEN THEM LAY **MEDUSA**...
...ASLEEP! I MUST ACT **QUICKLY**.
TURN AROUND AND BACK UP SLOWLY...
PERSEUS USED THE INSIDE OF THE SHIELD AS A MIRROR.
...JUST LIKE ATHENA TOLD ME TO.
THE ONLY SAFE WAY TO GAZE UPON...

...MEDUSA'S FACE!

AWAKE?!

SSSSSSSSSSSSS

SSSSSSSSSSSSSS!

SHE LUNGED TOWARD HIM...

...AND PERSEUS SLICED.

THACK

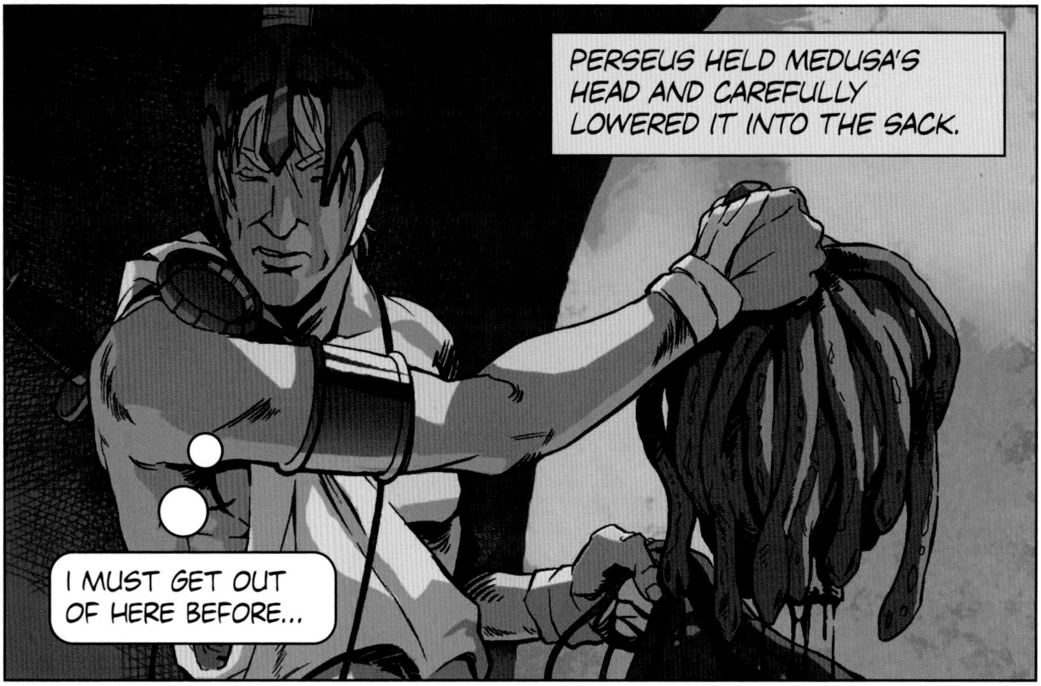
PERSEUS HELD MEDUSA'S HEAD AND CAREFULLY LOWERED IT INTO THE SACK.
I MUST GET OUT OF HERE BEFORE...

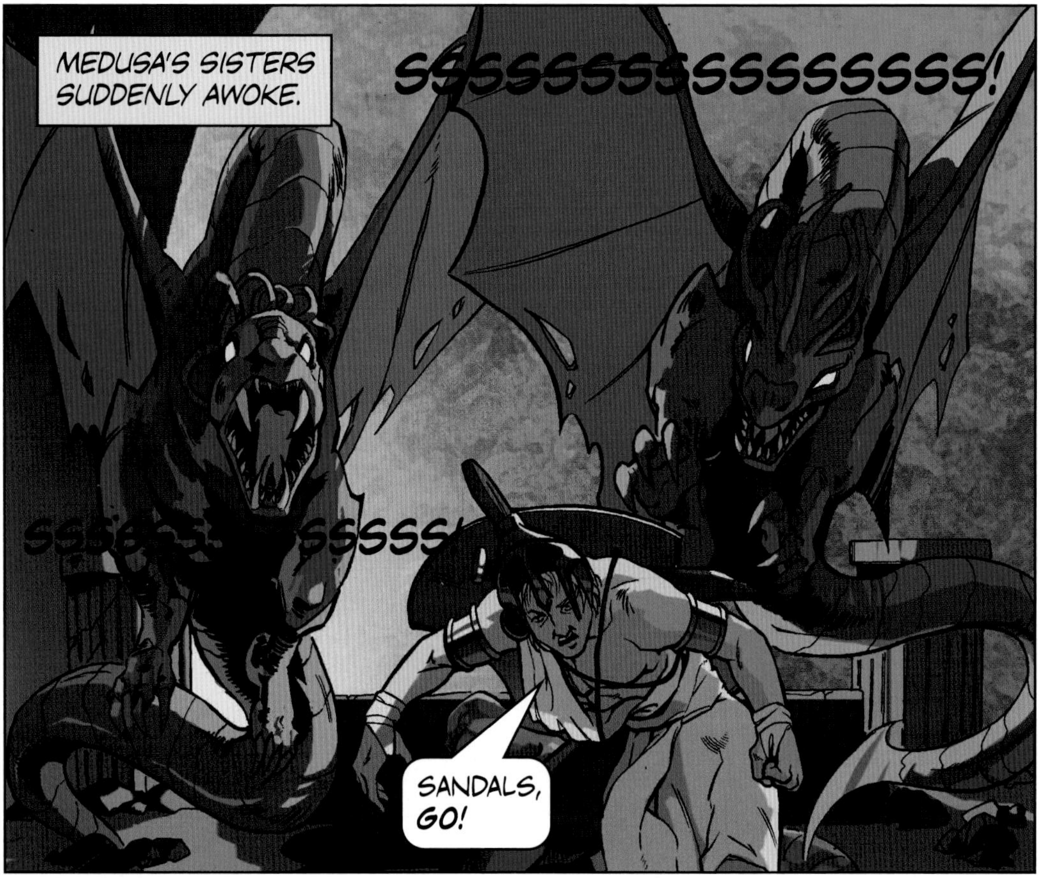
MEDUSA'S SISTERS SUDDENLY AWOKE.
SSSSSSSSSSSSSSSSSS!
SANDALS, GO!

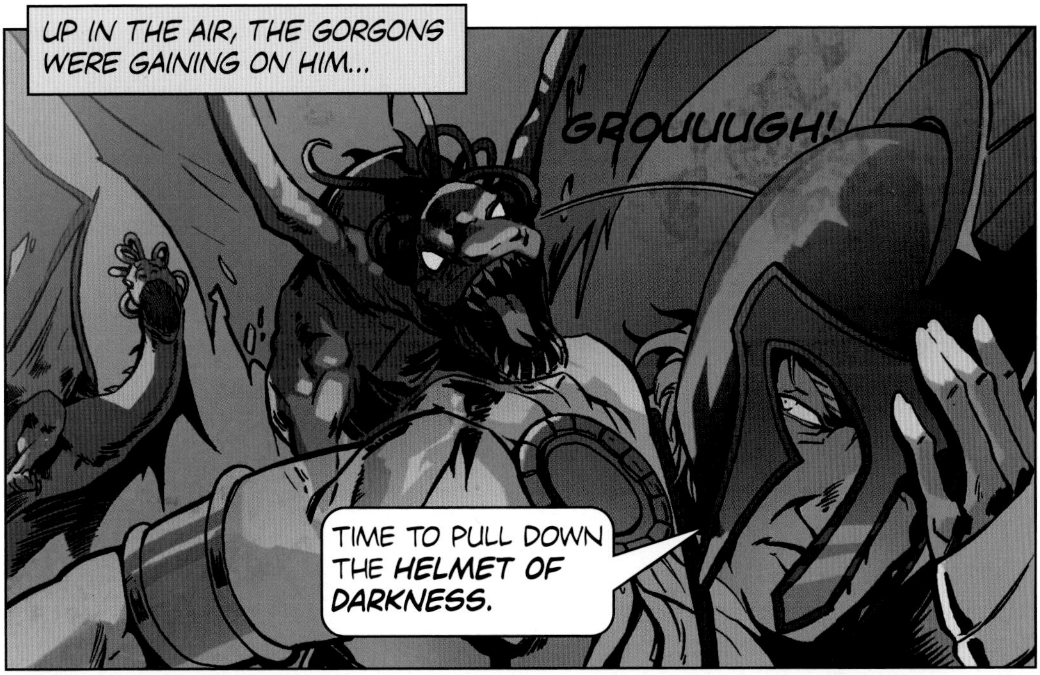
UP IN THE AIR, THE GORGONS WERE GAINING ON HIM...
GROUUUGH!
TIME TO PULL DOWN THE HELMET OF DARKNESS.

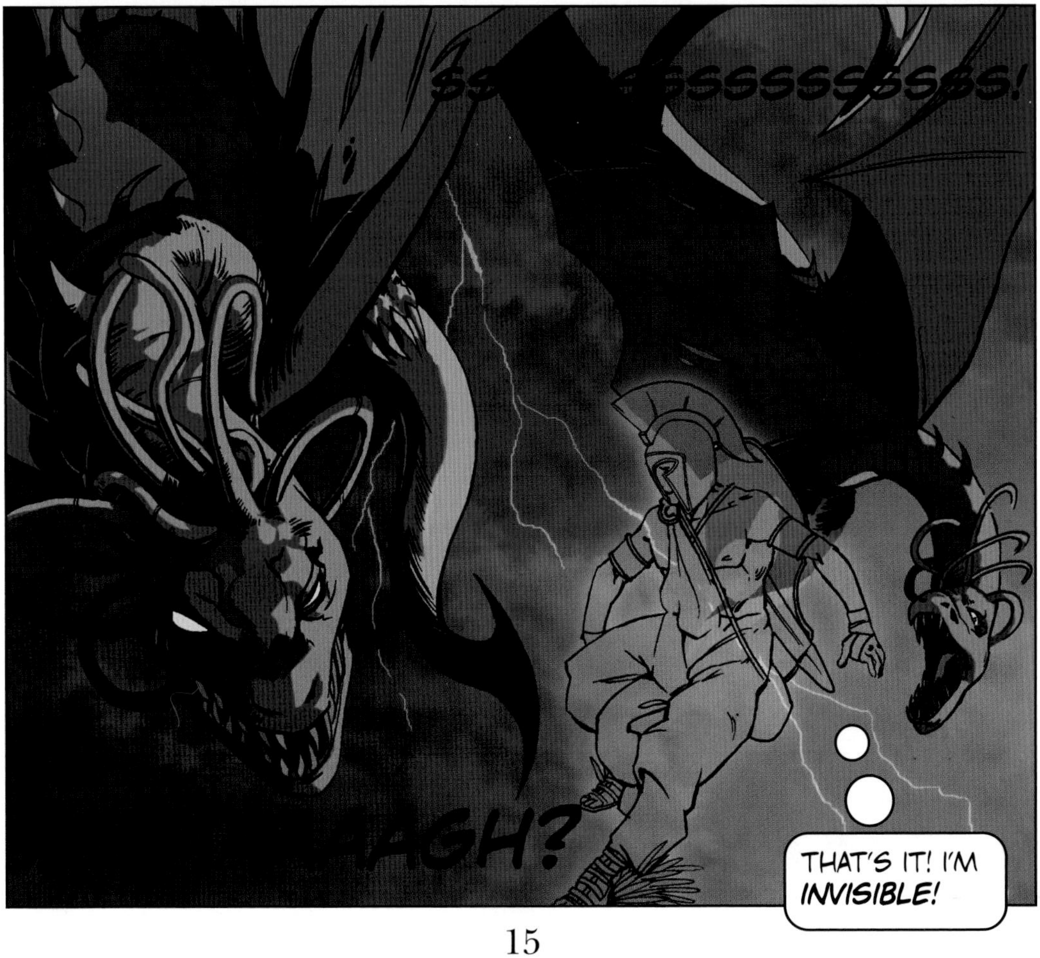
THAT'S IT! I'M INVISIBLE!

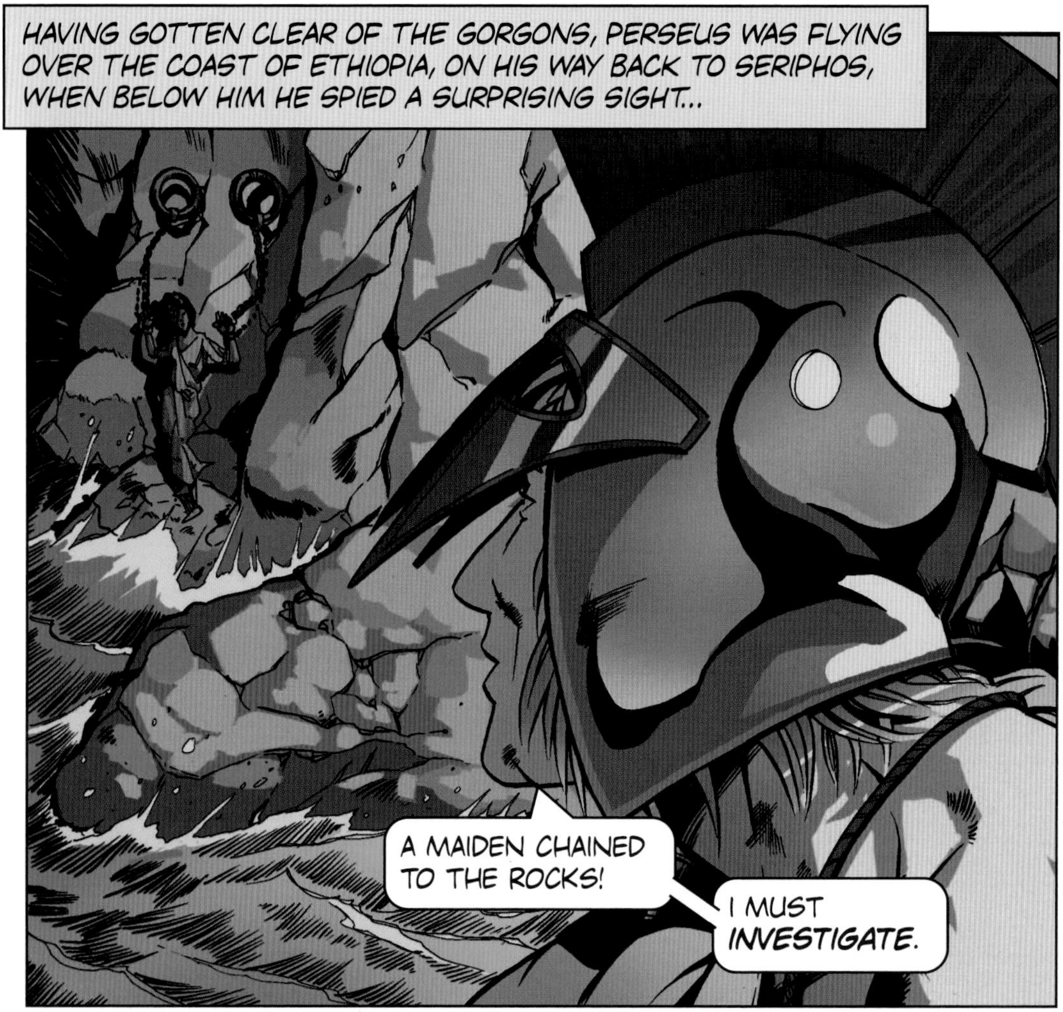
HAVING GOTTEN CLEAR OF THE GORGONS, PERSEUS WAS FLYING OVER THE COAST OF ETHIOPIA, ON HIS WAY BACK TO SERIPHOS, WHEN BELOW HIM HE SPIED A SURPRISING SIGHT...
A MAIDEN CHAINED TO THE ROCKS!
I MUST **INVESTIGATE**.

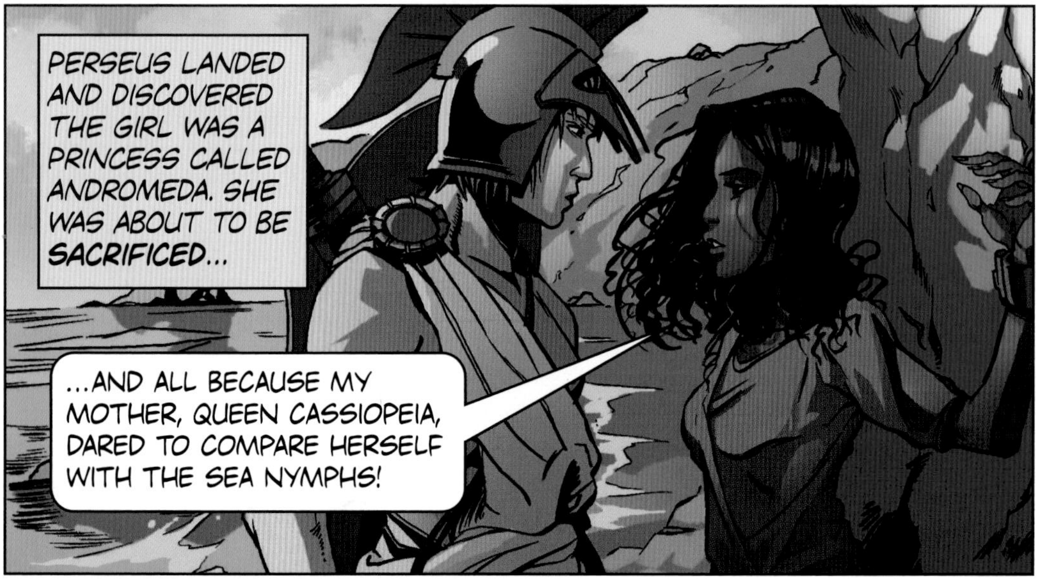
PERSEUS LANDED AND DISCOVERED THE GIRL WAS A PRINCESS CALLED ANDROMEDA. SHE WAS ABOUT TO BE **SACRIFICED**...
...AND ALL BECAUSE MY MOTHER, QUEEN CASSIOPEIA, DARED TO COMPARE HERSELF WITH THE SEA NYMPHS!

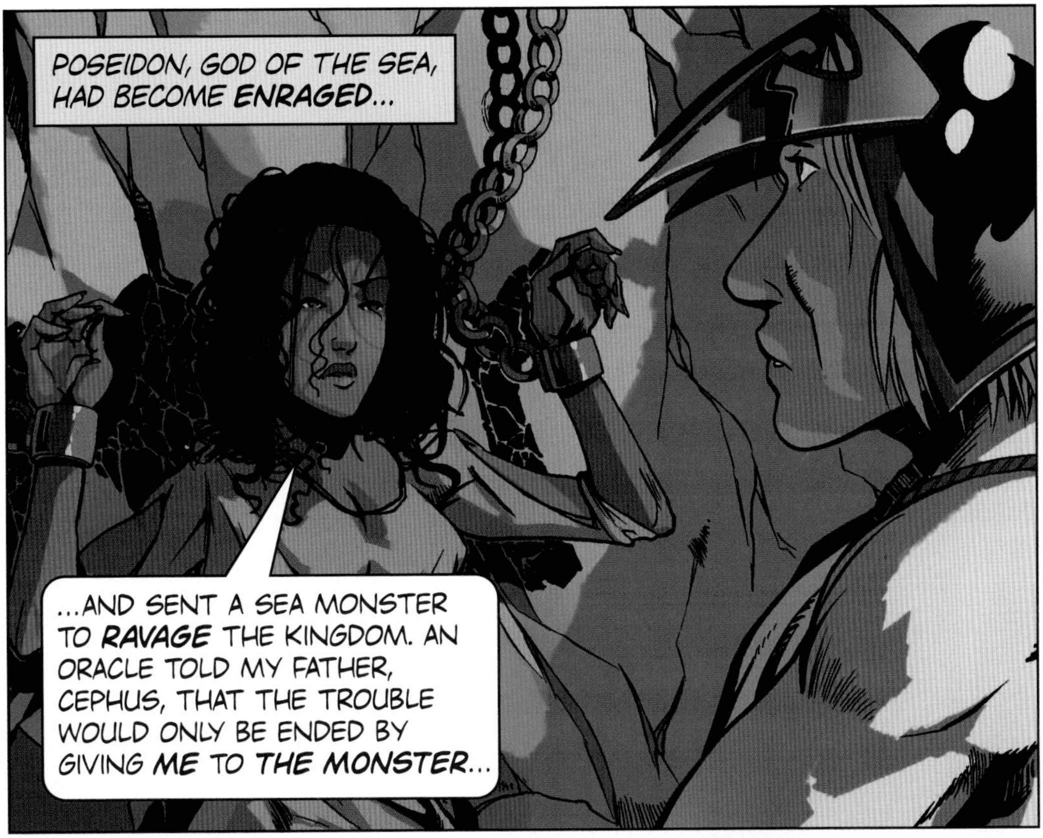
POSEIDON, GOD OF THE SEA, HAD BECOME ENRAGED...
...AND SENT A SEA MONSTER TO RAVAGE THE KINGDOM. AN ORACLE TOLD MY FATHER, CEPHUS, THAT THE TROUBLE WOULD ONLY BE ENDED BY GIVING ME TO THE MONSTER...

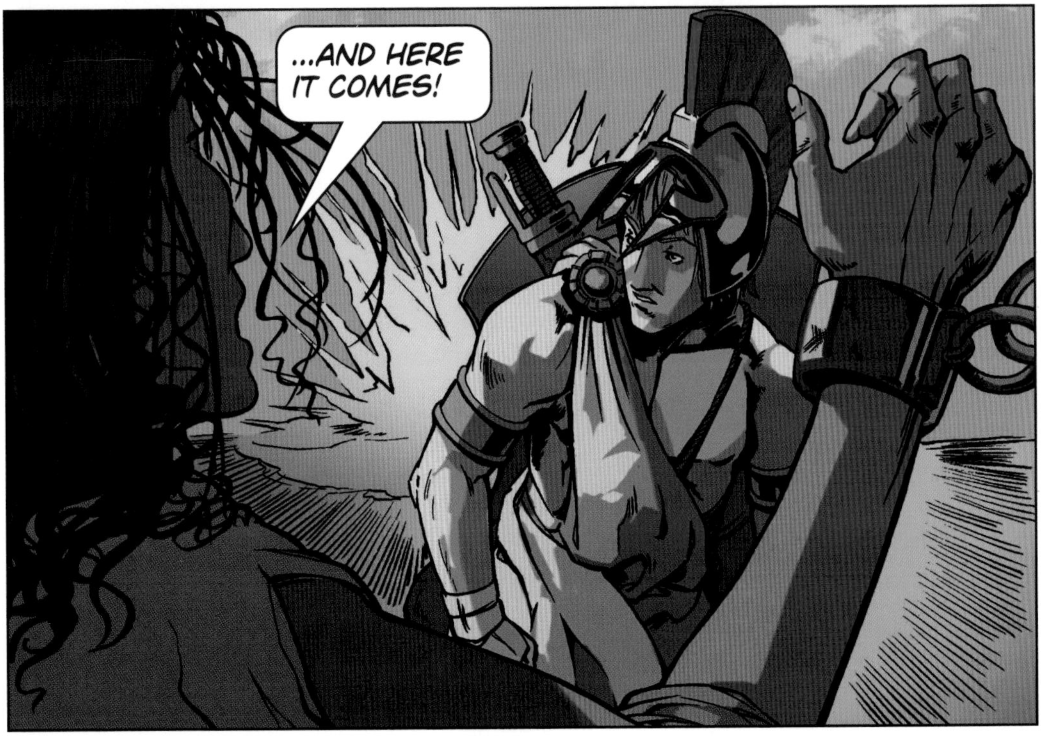
...AND HERE IT COMES!

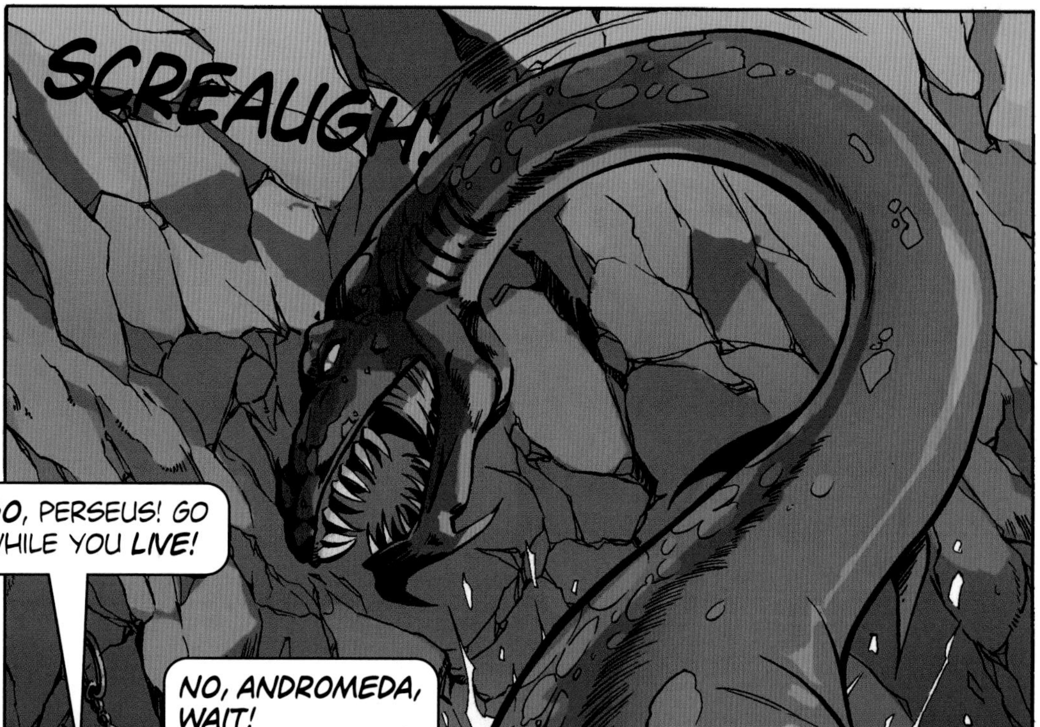
SCREAUGH!
GO, PERSEUS! GO WHILE YOU LIVE!
NO, ANDROMEDA, WAIT!

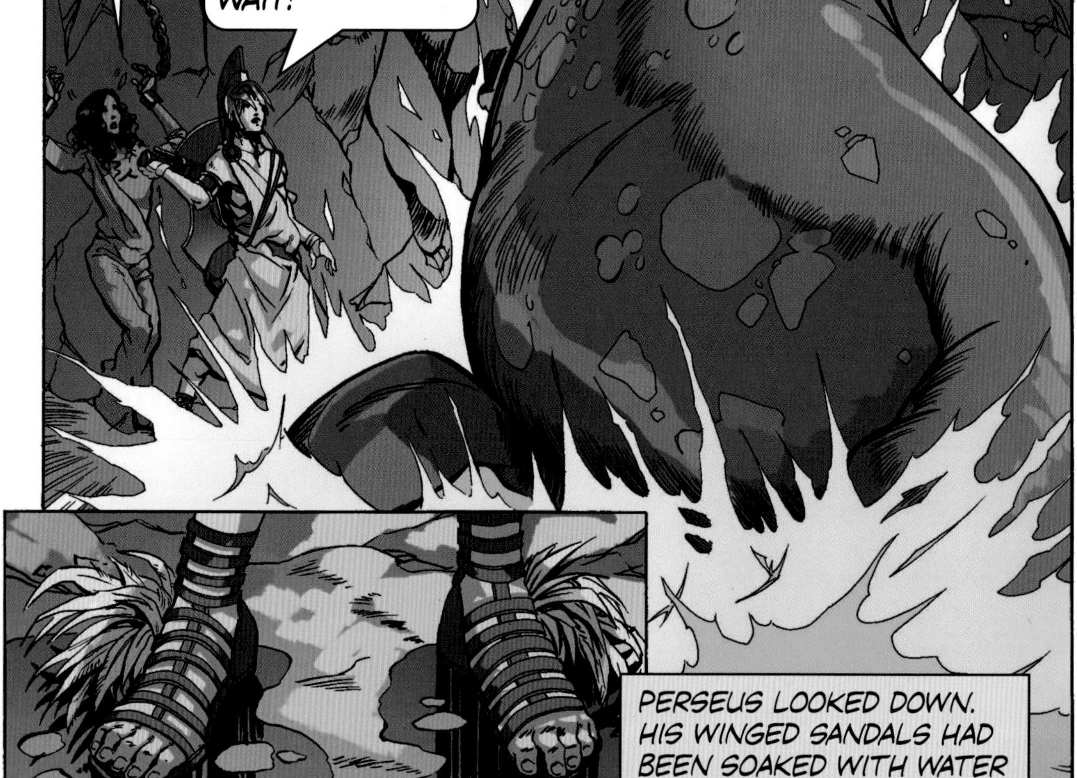
PERSEUS LOOKED DOWN. HIS WINGED SANDALS HAD BEEN SOAKED WITH WATER AND WERE USELESS.

SCREEEEEEEEEEEEEE!

HE REACHED QUICKLY INTO THE SACK.

LOOK AWAY! WHATEVER YOU DO, DON'T OPEN YOUR EYES!

HE HELD MEDUSA'S HEAD UP TO THE MONSTER'S GAZE.

SSSSSSSSSSSSSS!

SCREE?

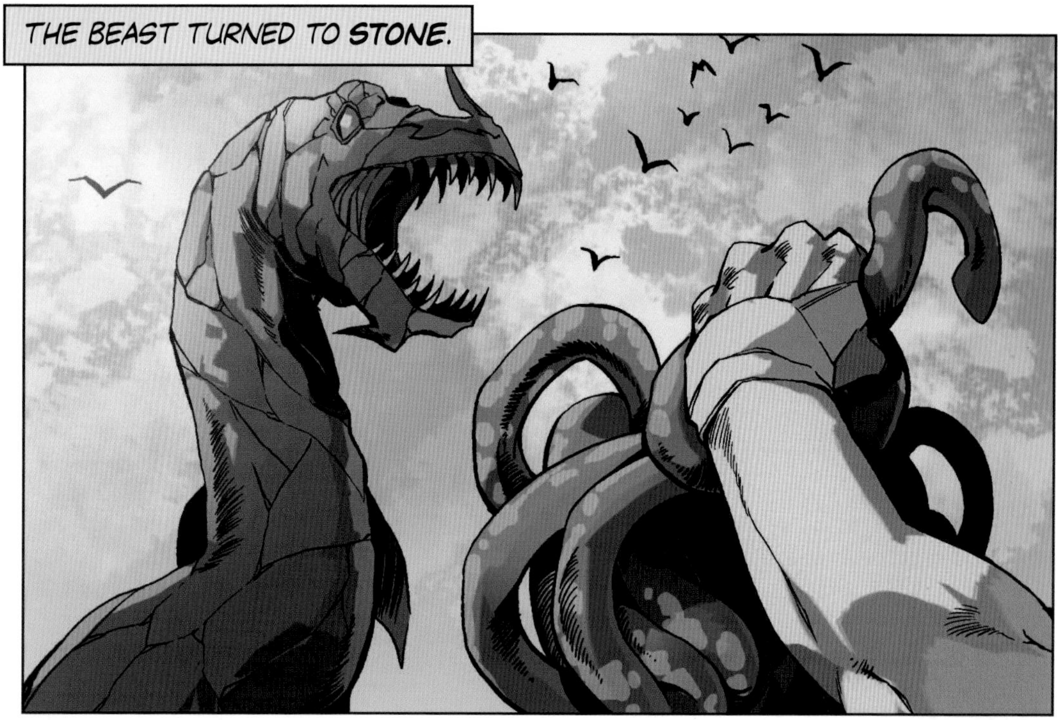
THE BEAST TURNED TO STONE.

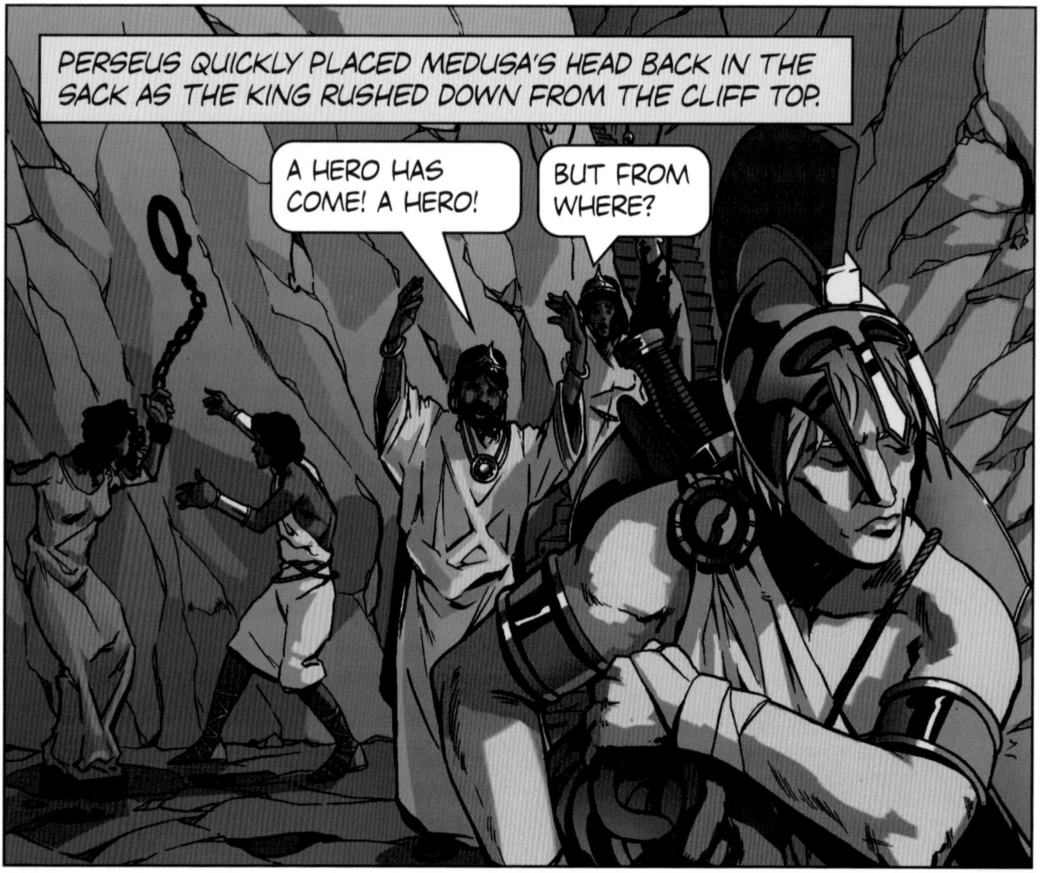
PERSEUS QUICKLY PLACED MEDUSA'S HEAD BACK IN THE SACK AS THE KING RUSHED DOWN FROM THE CLIFF TOP.
A HERO HAS COME! A HERO!
BUT FROM WHERE?

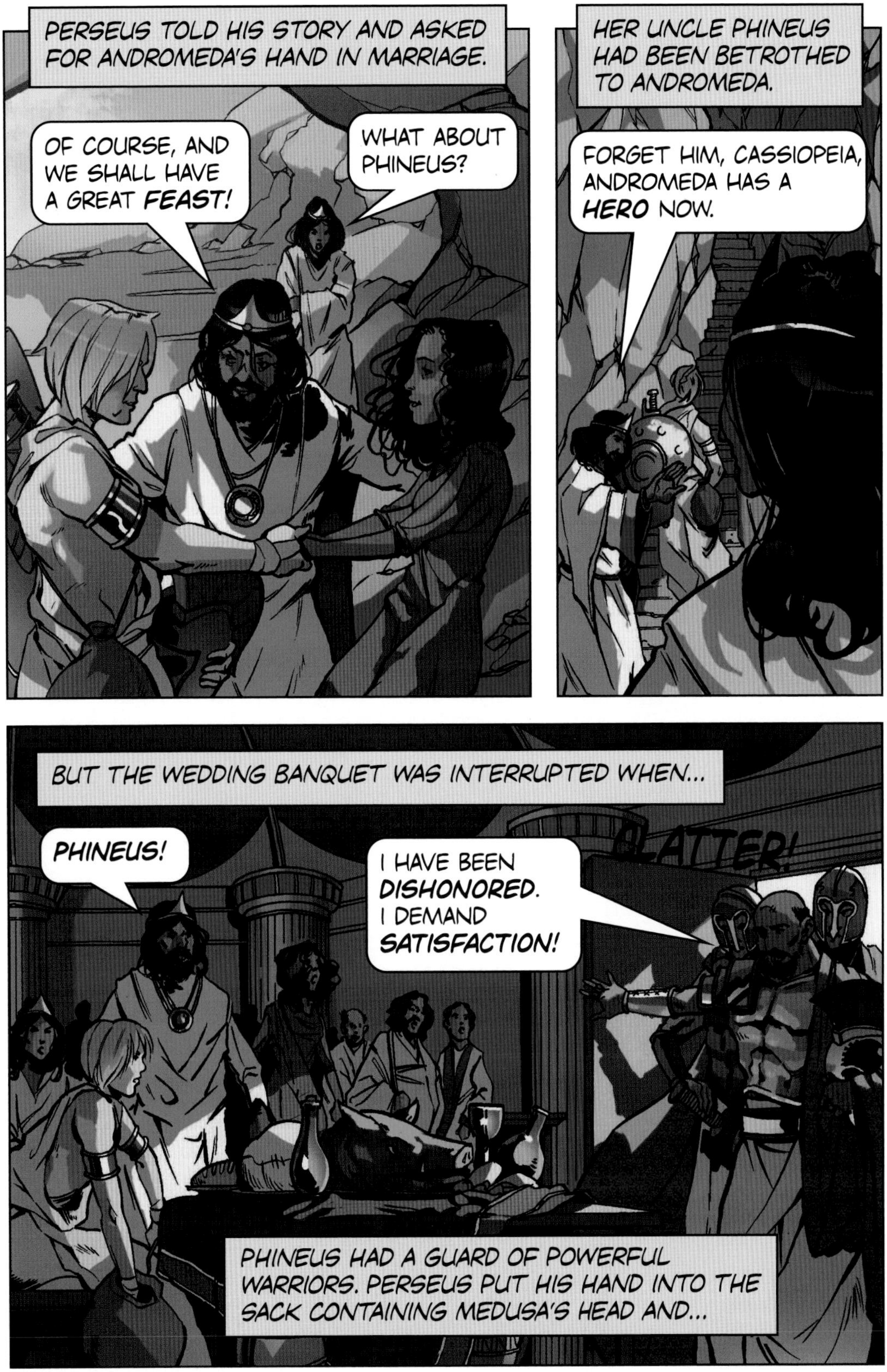

PERSEUS TOLD HIS STORY AND ASKED FOR ANDROMEDA'S HAND IN MARRIAGE.
OF COURSE, AND WE SHALL HAVE A GREAT **FEAST**!
WHAT ABOUT PHINEUS?
HER UNCLE PHINEUS HAD BEEN BETROTHED TO ANDROMEDA.
FORGET HIM, CASSIOPEIA, ANDROMEDA HAS A **HERO** NOW.
BUT THE WEDDING BANQUET WAS INTERRUPTED WHEN...
PHINEUS!
I HAVE BEEN **DISHONORED**. I DEMAND **SATISFACTION!**
PHINEUS HAD A GUARD OF POWERFUL WARRIORS. PERSEUS PUT HIS HAND INTO THE SACK CONTAINING MEDUSA'S HEAD AND...

Perseus shouted for the wedding guests to shield their eyes. The first of Phineus's soldiers stepped forward and met Medusa's gaze. He started back in alarm and moved no more. One by one, the soldiers became statues of stone, until Phineus dropped to his knees, and turning his head away, begged for mercy.

Pity Is for Fools

Perseus moved Medusa's head to the side to stare Phineus in the face, freezing him forever into a statue of a craven coward.

While Perseus was away, Polydectes had continued to press his attentions on Danae, and when she refused, had made her a slave. Perseus carried his bride to Seriphos on winged feet and asked Polydectes if he would like to see Medusa's head. The foolish king said yes and was turned to stone on his throne.

Final Reckoning

Perseus made Dictys king and gave Medusa's head to Athena as a prize. With Andromeda as his queen, he went on to found Mycene. One day, he was invited to take part in games at Argos. When he threw the discus, it went off course and struck old Acrisius in the head, killing him. And so the prophecy was fulfilled —the destroyer had triumphed.

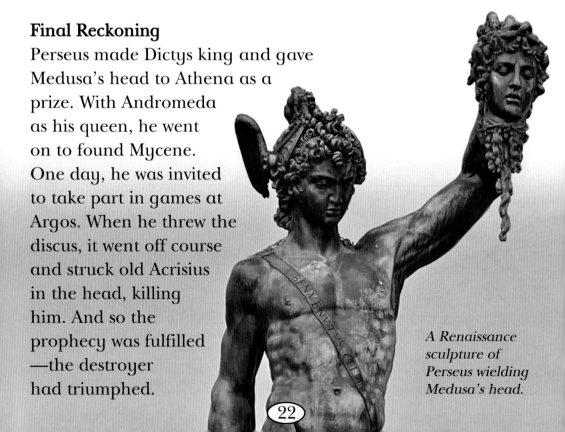

A Renaissance sculpture of Perseus wielding Medusa's head.

betrothed Engaged, promised to be married.

breastplate The front piece of a suit of armor that covers the chest.

craven Completely lacking courage.

crones Ugly old women.

discus A heavy, flattened object used in competitions to see who can throw it the farthest.

investigate To examine or gather more information.

lair The resting place of a wild animal or a place for hiding.

mocked Insulted, made fun of.

mortal Able to die.

oracle A person through whom a god speaks.

prophecy A prediction about the future.

ravage To attack, damage, and destroy.

woo To try to win a person's love.

INDEX